21 DAYS TO LIVING YOUR BEST LIFE

OMEGA'S
legacy

21 Days to Living Your Best Life

Published by: Omega's Legacy Publishing,

www.deshannonspeaks.org

First Edition, November 2014

Contact the Author

Connect with DeShannon Dixon at speaking@ deshannonspeaks.org visit her Website at www. deshannonspeaks.org

Dedication

To my husband Dave, and my children Keena, Zion, and Dayvid, if you can dream it - you can be it - thank you.

To the best siblings in the world Hoyt and Sharon, your support means everything.

To my cousin Kanika, without you my days would be boring. I love you.

INTRODUCTION

This 21-day devotional was written to inspire you, encourage you, and to make you think.

It also gives you a glimpse of how I have changed my thinking. I want everyone to LIVE your BEST LIFE. Today is a great day to do better, get stronger, and to believe that you can.

This isn't a 'stand on your head', 'turn around three times' and your life will change book, but it is one that will help you to re-evaluate your life's choices and decide that life is just not that bad.

To everyone who keeps praying for me or against me - thank you. I love you all.

Hugs and Blessings

DeShannon Bynum Dixon

PS. Before you start reading, get yourself a notebook or use the notes section. I want to encourage you to write and journal your walk through this devotional.

Do you have to do this - NO, but I would like you to (smile).

Day 1

You Get What You Say

Proverbs 18:21 NLT The tongue can bring death or life; those who love to talk will reap its consequences.

Have you ever paid much attention to the words that come out of your mouth?

Take a moment and think about everything you've said today? Was it positive, negative, meaningful, hateful, belittling, or encouraging?Maybe what you've said was a combination of them all.

What if you actually THOUGHT about what you said BEFORE the words come out of your mouth. You my not always be able to control your thoughts but you can certainly control your words.

Have you ever said "this is the worst day ever" and the day just became unbearable. Or "I feel horrible" and no matter what you did you felt horrible. Well folks you got exactly what you said. How about when it comes to your finances? Ever said " let me save for a rainy day" and every time you get a little money saved IT RAINS. The car needs fixing, an unexpected bill, unexpected RAIN!

Imagine if you had said "this is the best day ever" or "I feel great" or "I always have enough money" Sounds simple doesn't it.

It takes practice. Why not start today!

Isaiah 55:11 NLT says, "It is the same with my word. I send it out and it always produces fruit. It will accomplish all I want it to, and it will prosper everywhere I send it".

If God lives inside you (your heart) then whatever you say "produces fruit" and "prospers"
So begin to declare what you want to produce FRUIT!

THINK ABOUT IT. . . .

Think about today's words, write down everything you can remember saying that was negative. Now draw a line through them. You have just cancelled those things out.

Now write down things you WANT to produce fruit (things you want to happen)

Ex: I have everything I need, I feel great today, I'm blessed everyday, I am _____

NOTES:

_____

_____

_____

_____

_____

_____

Day 2

WITHHOLDING NOTHING

Psalms 84:11 NLT says "For the LORD God is our sun and our shield. He gives us grace and glory. The LORD will withhold no good thing from those who do what is right."

God knows exactly what we need and if it's good for us we can have it.

Problem is we are too busy holding on to things that are simply NO GOOD.

We want to tell God what's best for us, whether it be in a relationship, friends, or jobs.

We want what we want, and when God tells us NO, we are offended! Often questioning "did I hear that right" If I prayed about it, doesn't God answer our prayer?!

We make all kinds of excuses as to why things just don't work out. It usually has blame involved. We love to blame any and everybody for a downfall.

Pump your brakes a minute! Could the "it didn't work out" just be that it was **NO GOOD!**

Begin to think back at your disappointments and what you initially thought was a failure, if we believe God's word is true then we can

REJOICE in knowing THE LORD WILL WITHHOLD NO GOOD THING FROM YOU!!!

It is a blow to our EGO to come to grips with the fact that we can't make our own best decisions. We need God's help. If we simply ask God "is this a good thing for me" before we do anything, we wouldn't have as many disappointments.

THINK ABOUT IT. . . .

What are some things that you know God has told or shown you that are NO GOOD. Write those things down. Look at them. Now cross them out, thank God that he didn't let you have everything you thought you wanted.

NOTES:

_____

_____

_____

_____

_____

_____

_____

_____

Day 3

IT IS OK TO TELL

James 5:16 New Living Translation (NLT) "Confess your sins to each other and pray for each other so that you may be healed. The earnest prayer of a righteous person has great power and produces wonderful results.

One main reason we only to talk about the last part of this scripture is that we have trust issues. How often have we been betrayed by those people we confided in?

This reminds us to pray for each other, so that healing can take place. Healing from what? Healing from sickness, pain, disappointment, hurt, mistrust, and lies the list can go on.

No one wants to be perceived as BAD or the one who has done terrible things. We often forget ALL have sinned. There are no levels to sin. Sin is Sin.

I encourage you to find someone you trust to hold you accountable, to pray with you to check in with you.

Studies show that when starting to a new exercise plan it is more successful when you have a partner. There will be days when one partner needs a little encouragement to get up and complete that workout. It's the same with our walk (exercise) with Christ. You need a prayer partner holding you up in prayer when you just don't feel like you can make it.

Think About It....

Write down something you have been through that may help someone with a similar situation. How would you feel telling your testimony?

Notes:

_____

_____

_____

_____

_____

_____

_____

_____

_____

_____

_____

_____

_____

_____

Day 4

At All Times

Psalm 34:1 King James Version (KJV) "I will bless the Lord at all times: his praise shall continually be in my mouth."

What is coming out of your mouth? Are you blessing (adoring, praising, lifting up) the name of The Lord in the good AND the bad times?

At all times doesn't mean on Sunday during service, or when a prayer has suddenly been answered. It means even in the dark times, the quiet times, the times of uncertainty.

How would our lives change if we blessed The Lord at all times? In spite of the situation I will constantly speak of how good you are.

I will remind myself day and night of how good you have been to me.

I will look back over each day and recognize the areas in my life that you showed up and took care of me. I will constantly tell other people of your love for me.

Think About It. . . .

What has God done for you today? Write a list. Now thank him for EACH thing on your list.

Notes:

_____

_____

_____

_____

_____

_____

_____

_____

_____

_____

_____

_____

_____

_____

_____

_____

_____

_____

_____

Day 5

I<small>T</small>'<small>S</small> N<small>OT</small> Y<small>OUR</small> F<small>IGHT</small>

2 Chronicles 20:15 New International Version (NIV)
"Do not be afraid or discouraged because of this vast army. For the battle is not yours, but God's".

Our greatest battles are already won. We never have to get inside the ring. We get to watch from ringside.

God has declared he will fight our battles for us. We only have two things to do.

(1) Remain calm and
(2) get out of the way.

The moment we step into the ring we tell God, "We got this", "We don't need your help".

God wants us to trust HIS corner, (Jesus/Holy Spirit)
He needs for us to cheer (praise) him from the side.

Another thing we must do is to continue to pray for our opponent, they really need to know when to throw in the towel. They have already LOST and don't even know it.

Notes:

_____

_____

_____

_____

_____

_____

_____

_____

_____

_____

_____

_____

_____

_____

_____

_____

_____

Day 6
YOUR PAST HAS A PURPOSE

Galatians 6:1 New International Version (NIV) "Brothers and sisters, if someone is caught in a sin, you who live by the Spirit should restore that person gently. But watch yourselves, or you also may be tempted."

Telling the goodness of Jesus or "giving your testimony" used to be something of pride. You wanted everyone to know where God has brought you from. This is a lost art. We shy away from our testimony because somewhere along the lines we have begun to tell ourselves "I'm not telling people my business"

There is a passage in the bible where the disciples describe Mary Magdalene as the one that had seven demons cast out of her.

There will always be someone "throwing up" your past. Reminding you of where you came from. I encourage you to own your past. It has taught you some very valuable lessons, ones that if told will help someone going through and if we are lucky will STOP someone from making the same mistakes.

I'm not suggesting every time you get a chance you have to be the first one up giving the most intimate details of your past. But listen careful to the Holy Spirit he will let you know when and where to proudly declare just where God has brought you through.

THINK ABOUT IT....

Have you forgiven yourself for your past?
Do you feel people will look at your different if they knew your "story"?

Write down the worse thing you've done, its ok no one will see your notebook but you. Now draw a line through it. Cancel it; God forgave you- and you just forgiven yourself.

Notes:

Day 7

HURT FEELINGS

Matthew 5:44 New International Version (NIV) "But I tell you, love your enemies and pray for those who persecute you".

When someone hurts our feelings...
Frankly it SUCKS!
When I started asking myself WHY does it hurt?

Often we hurt because someone did something that we wouldn't do, or didn't do something we expected them to do - either way because we couldn't control what someone else chose to do OUR feelings became bruised.

I'm praying that you accept that people DON'T have to do what you think they should... And it perfectly ok!! Begin to ask God to heal your bruised feeling and bless the person you've tried to control. Not what you were expecting me to type: I know-I know

Wait!!!! Are you saying I am trying to control the person who HURT ME?? That's exactly what I am saying.

We expect people that we are close to (and sometimes not so close to) to have the same views and values as ourselves NEWS FLASH - they don't. This is where hurt comes in.

We are hurt because we don't UNDERSTAND WHY!
Why they did/didn't do this to me. Even if the offender offers an expla-

nation - the excuse is never acceptable further wounding our expectations.

Are you saying I shouldn't expect people NOT to hurt me?
No, what I am saying is your expectation may not line up with their actions.

Everyone (including you) makes choices every second of every day. The freedom comes from not allowing someone else's action to wound you.

Every person you come in contact with will help you or will teach you, if it is a teaching moment learn quickly so that you will not repeat this lesson again. If it is a helping moment - don't forget to give thanks for the blessing.

PRAYER :

Father, my feelings are hurt because of _____, I realize now that I have no control over another person's actions. I ask that you heal my broken heart and bless _____. I give all my emotions over to you. Amen.

Do you feel people will look at your different if they knew.

NOTES :

_____

_____

_____

_____

Day 8

CALL HIM UP

Psalm 18:3 New International Version (NIV) "I called to the Lord, who is worthy of praise, and I have been saved from my enemies".

I hear a lot of times people say they don't know how to pray. We all learned "Our Father which art in heaven" prayer. **But is this different?** I'm not talking about learned church behavior. I am talking about having a conversation with God.

Often it takes "folks messing with us" before we feel the need to talk to God. No, this isn't the only time we come to God but it's in the top five.

When we have enemies - or opposers, we often feel hopeless, small even, unable to stand tall and confront this life-size giant. We have made our enemies bigger than our GOD. In these times call to The Lord.
Cast your care on the Christ within, He is able to handle any kind of trouble we face.

He is worthy of praise, He has never failed you, He is your father. He will save you from your enemy even if that enemy is yourself. All you have to do is call out to him, he is waiting on you. It's not hard, it's easy, just open your heart and let him help you.

THINK ABOUT IT....

Write out what you need God to help you with.

Do you have any enemies? List those people; beside their names tell what they have done to you. Now ask God to help you forgive them.

NOTES:

_____

_____

_____

_____

_____

_____

_____

_____

_____

_____

_____

_____

_____

_____

_____

Day 9

TIME TO EAT

Psalm 23:5 New King James Version (NKJV)
"You prepare a table before me in the presence of my enemies;"

Anytime someone is preparing a table that can only mean one thing-it's time to eat. But why do I have to eat with my enemies around? And just what are we eating?

We often look at "haters" as bad things. These are people who "get under your skin" they often try to turn people against you by spreading rumors or creating discord. They try to starve you out.

They may try, but scripture tells us No weapon formed against us shall prosper. It just won't work.

When God blesses you he lets everyone know. (They get to watch). They often cannot believe you made it through your situation. They only get a Birdseye view.

They get to SEE just how good God has been to you. They get to see you eating the blessings of God.

PRAYER:

Lord, there are people who may want me to fail but I put all my trust in you. I understand that the weapons formed against me will not work. I thank you for being with me in this difficult time. Amen

Notes:

Day 10

WANTING NOTHING

Psalm 23:1New King James Version (NKJV) 23 The Lord is my shepherd; I shall not want.

Most people who believe in God love to quote this scripture. It's often said to be a comforting scripture. I must agree it is a favorite of mine as well.

When I teach Bible Study which I have renamed CROSSTraining at my local church I try to take a fresh approach to tackling the scriptures.

"The Lord is my shepherd; I shall not want"

Could we say IF you follow God you can have everything you WANT? The NIV says: *"The Lord is my Shepard; I lack nothing"* So why are we seemingly in LACK? Why are we constantly asking God for something, anything, and everything?

Have we forgotten the first part of the scripture? WE HAVE TO FOLLOW the shepherd! Then we can confidently declare the 2nd part of the scripture.

I CAN HAVE WHAT I WANT!

THINK ABOUT IT. . . .

What do you WANT? Make a list

Now go back to the scripture, follow God and you can have what you want.

NOTES

_____

_____

_____

_____

_____

_____

_____

_____

_____

_____

_____

_____

_____

_____

_____

Day 11

Overflow Blessings

Malachi 3:10King James Version (KJV)
"Bring ye all the tithes into the storehouse, that there may be meat in mine house, and prove me now herewith, saith the Lord of hosts, if I will not open you the windows of heaven, and pour you out a blessing, that there shall not be room enough to receive it."

We love the "open up the windows and pour out a blessing" part of the scripture. But tend to shy away from the "bring ye all the tithe" part.

> We make every excuse for not giving our tithe.
> When actually there is no excuse NOT to give.
> We want overflow blessings without giving. We make excuses when there isn't any. We find a way NOT to give.

I want overflow blessings, I want to make room for my blessings, I want more than enough.

Prayer:

Lord, I believe your word is true. As I give a 10th of what you have given me I can expect it to return to me in overflow. Amen

Think About It...

Go get your paycheck, are you giving 10%?
If not, let's work on doing better; give one per

NOTES:

Day 12

Old Wise One

Proverbs 3:7 New International Version (NIV)
"Do not be wise in your own eyes; fear the Lord and shun evil."

Every one of us has felt the need to be RIGHT, our way was better than someone else's.
We have even given unsolicited advice.

I'm right and you're wrong!
A sense of pride tends to flood over us at the thought of " I told you so"

I caution you in this. Did we seek God before we gave our advice? Have we taken credit for advice that wasn't God ordained? Have we traded the voice of God for "it's my way or the highway?"

Wisdom comes from God.

Wisdom knows what to do; knowledge knows when to do it.

Prayer

Father, forgive me for being quick to give my opinion without seeking you first. Wisdom is knowing what to do and knowledge is knowing when to do it. Let me always seek you first and not depend on my own thinking. Amen

NOTES

_____

_____

_____

_____

_____

_____

_____

_____

_____

_____

_____

_____

_____

_____

_____

_____

_____

_____

Day 13

GET SOME REST

Matthew 11:28 New International Version (NIV) "Come to me, all you who are weary and burdened, and I will give you rest."

Jesus wants to carry your burdens for you. We have NO trouble bringing our problems to The Lord, but as soon as we say AMEN, we have picked them back up and begin to worry again.

We cannot carry our burdens. They're just too heavy. We have no idea if we are even going to wake up in the morning. So why not give our problems to the only one who holds the future?

Then and only then can we have REST.

Wouldn't it be nice to REST, I mean really rest. You can have the rest you deserve. It's waiting on you.

Prayer:
Father, I need you, I can't carry these problems any longer. I need you to help me. I need to rest. So I give you this burden of _____
and I can rest knowing that you are able to work this out for my good. Amen

THINK ABOUT IT...

What burdens are you carrying? Write them down. Now cross them off as you give each of them to Christ.

NOTES:

_____

_____

_____

_____

_____

_____

_____

_____

_____

_____

_____

_____

_____

_____

_____

_____

Day 14

WRITE IT DOWN

Habakkuk 2:2 King James Version (KJV) "And the Lord answered me, and said, Write the vision, and make it plain upon tables!"

There is something inside of us that needs to be written down!

When you write things down it helps you visualize your goals.

Have you ever gone to the grocery store without a list???
A complete cluster, right???
Without a list we usually end up with more than what we need and forget the very thing you went in for.

BUT a list keeps us on track. It helps us stay focused. We have a guide.

GET OUT YOUR NOTEBOOK

I encourage you to write down your dreams, goals and prayers. Use it as a guideline to accomplish what you set out to do.

NOTES

_____

_____

_____

_____

_____

_____

_____

_____

_____

_____

_____

_____

_____

_____

_____

_____

_____

Day 15

Wearing Your Heart

Psalm 37:4 New King James Version (NKJV) "Delight yourself also in the Lord, And He shall give you the desires of your heart."

Which loosely translate (the DeShannon version)
Respect God and live according to his ways, and you can have EVERYTHING you want.

What does your heart desire?

We often hide what's in our heart, never wearing our heart on our sleeves. Never being transparent enough to share our hopes and dreams with anyone. Sometimes not even trusting ourselves with our BIG WISHES.

We often believe our hearts desires will never be achieved so we dismiss them as fleeting thoughts.

I want to wear my heart on my sleeve. I want to share my desires. I want you to love or hate me. I am just tired of hiding. I want to respect God and his ways enough to ask once and it shall be! Doubt not!

Does this also mean I don't have the desires of my heart if I don't follow God? Am I the hold up on my dreams and desires? My books, my business, my speaking engagements, my millions are being held up because of me??

My heart's desire is to be pleasing to my Heavenly Father, and all things will be added to me.

Praying that the desires of your heart are given to you SUDDENLY without delay

GET OUT YOUR NOTEBOOK

What do you desire?

NOTES

_____

_____

_____

_____

_____

_____

_____

_____

_____

_____

_____

Day 16

In Due Time

Galatians 6:9 NLT
"So let's not get tired of doing what is good. At just the right time we will reap a harvest of blessings if we don't give up"

"If we don't give up?" Why would we want to give up "doing what is good?"
Could it be that we are focused on people around us doing wrong in our eyes.

Psalms 37:1-2 NLT
"Don't worry about the wicked or envy those who do wrong. For like grass, they soon fade away."

Let me get this straight...
I'm supposed to keep doing good and wait for my blessings while THEY get away with murder and IN DUE TIME they will fade away....

Well, YES!

We spend way too much time worrying about the fate of other people. Let's focus on reaping the harvest of blessing so we won't be the ones fading away.

NOTES

_____

_____

_____

_____

_____

_____

_____

_____

_____

_____

_____

_____

_____

_____

_____

_____

_____

_____

Day 17

Run Your Race

Philippians 3:14New International Version (NIV)
"I press on toward the goal to win the prize for which God has called
me heavenward in Christ Jesus."

Have you heard the expression "stay in your lane" which loosely translates into "mind your own business or worry about your own affairs?"

I want to encourage you to run your own race. You are uniquely made and qualified to finish the race that is set out for you. You may not start when the pistol fires or finish in someone else's qualifying heat but if you run your own race you will finish and you will WIN!

We can easily be persuaded to run someone else's race, usually out of fear that we may be on the track alone, at a time when there seems to be odds stacked against us, but that's when you allow the wind to push you forward.

This is where "stay in your lane" applies...

This is your race, you cannot concern yourself with what you feel is competition. There is no competition in God. He has given each of us a gift that belongs ONLY to us. So it doesn't matter who is ahead of you or behind you. ONLY you can run this race.

So let me encourage you.

Get Up, Get Going, take a water break if you need to; but RUN!
The finish line is waiting for you, and guess what? The PRIZE is better than you could ever imagine.

NOTES

_____

_____

_____

_____

_____

_____

_____

_____

_____

_____

_____

_____

_____

_____

_____

_____

_____

Day 18

Under Construction

Philippians 1:6New International Version (NIV)
"Being confident of this, that he who began a good work in you will carry it on to completion until the day of Christ Jesus."

Everyone dreads construction. Before anything is remodeled it usually has to be torn down, space has to be cleared and junk hauled away. Then there is the noise! There is some type of disruption in the normal way things are done to MAKE way for the new! Sometimes it takes several years before one project is complete.

As soon as that job is complete another one begins. There may be several projects going on at once, but we put up with it because we know when it's finished it will be GREAT.

So it is with our lives, we are constantly under construction.

The scripture above lets me know GOD will be constantly working on us.
We are being remodeled to look more and be more like him. Some of the demolition will be painful, the tearing down of walls will be uncomfortable, but the finished product will be fantastic!

Think About It...

What are the areas God is still working on in your life?

NOTES

_____

_____

_____

_____

_____

_____

_____

_____

_____

_____

_____

_____

_____

_____

_____

_____

_____

_____

Day 19

MOVING MOUNTAINS

Matthew 17:20 New Living Translation (NLT) "You don't have enough faith," Jesus told them. "I tell you the truth, if you had faith even as small as a mustard seed, you could say to this mountain, Move from here to there, and it would move. Nothing would be impossible"

Why is it so hard to have FAITH when we only need a tiny bit in order to change our current situation? We read the scriptures and we believe that God can do the impossible but we sometimes have trouble believing WE can do the impossible as well.

I don't know about you but I need MOUNTAINS moved?
What are your mountains? What's in the way? What do you need moved.

Have you SPOKEN to the situation and demanded it to MOVE?
Have you declared fearlessly that God's word accomplishes what it set out to do?

If nothing is impossible with GOD and GOD is with you- then NOTH-ING is impossible with you either.

Begin to say, "This mountain _____ will move out of my way."

This statement settles it! This statement gives you BACK the power that

God gave you.

When you are no longer moved by mountains, mountains will move.

THINK ABOUT IT. . .

Write down the situations you need to MOVE out of your way.

NOTES

_____

_____

_____

_____

_____

_____

_____

_____

_____

_____

_____

_____

_____

Day 20

Do Not Look Back

Genesis 19:17 New Living Translation (NLT)
"When they were safely out of the city, one of the angels ordered, "Run for your lives! And don't look back or stop anywhere in the valley! Escape to the mountains, or you will be swept away!"

We often hear people say, "You can't move forward if you're constantly looking back". I get that...they want you to continue moving forward.

I am reminded that we often look back because we don't really want to leave what God is removing us from.

When God has removed us from relationships, jobs, towns etc. We often keep in contact with someone who can keep up informed on the "happenings" But I want to encourage you "don't look back"

There is nothing going on BACK there that concerns you, and keeping up with what God has already removed you from keeps you from advancing.

Remember the story of Noah? God didn't destroy the land until AFTER Noah was safe INSIDE the boat. God wants to protect us from the flood that's coming. You need to stay in the boat. Safe from harm.

Sodom and Gomorrah wasn't destroyed until after Abraham and family had left. They were warned NOT to look back. Well you know the story, when Lot's wife looked back she was turned into a pillar of salt.

Salt! That's what happens when we look back we get "salty" we continue to think about it, talk about it, replay it over and over until we are so salty we CAN'T move forward. We are like stone – unmovable, a pillar of salt!

Whatever is left behind, is left there for a reason, let God work that out.

Prayer :
Father, thank you for removing me from situations that were not good for me. I will look ahead at what you have promised me. I bless those things behind me. Amen

Notes

Day 21

No Matter What

Psalm 27:10 New Living Translation (NLT)
"Even if my father and mother abandon me, the Lord will hold me close."

Wow, we never expect our parents to abandon us. Not both of them, anyway. Many of us have been raised by only one parent, or maybe even a close family member, adoption, or foster care but we had SOMEBODY.

God lets us know that even if everyone we know turns their backs on us; he will always hold us close. He will wrap his loving arms around us and take care of us. He will never leave.

God loves you so much that he patiently waits for us to come to him. That's what you call family.

You have to accept that you, yes you, are a part of God's family and you have all the rights and privileges of his other children.

Think About It...

Have you ever felt abandoned? When?

NOTES

_____

_____

_____

_____

_____

_____

_____

_____

_____

_____

_____

_____

_____

_____

_____

_____

_____

Conclusion

<u>It Has Been 21 Days</u>

I pray that you have connected with the chapters in this devotional. Take a look back at your notebook and all the things you have written down. Do you realize God is concerned with everything that concerns you and he wants only the best for you.

You can have the life that is predestined for you to have. You can have everything that is yours by divine right. You can live better than good, beyond good.

You can live in peace by allowing God to lead you each and every day.

God doesn't expect you to be perfect, he expects you to lean and depend on him.

I am praying with you, I am believing with you

Your best life starts Now